50 Simply Sushi Recipes

By: Kelly Johnson

Table of Contents

- California Roll
- Spicy Tuna Roll
- Dragon Roll
- Rainbow Roll
- Philly Roll
- Shrimp Tempura Roll
- Ebi Nigiri
- Avocado Cucumber Roll
- Spider Roll
- Salmon and Avocado Roll
- Veggie Roll
- Tuna Nigiri
- Unagi (Grilled Eel) Roll
- Tempura Shrimp Nigiri
- Spider Roll with Soft Shell Crab
- Crispy Shrimp Roll
- Salmon Roe Gunkan Maki
- Tuna Tataki Roll
- Poke Roll
- Sashimi Salad Roll
- Spicy Crab Roll
- Tamago (Japanese Omelette) Nigiri
- Yellowtail Roll
- Maki Roll with Scallops
- Hamachi (Yellowtail) Nigiri
- Salmon Skin Roll
- Crab Stick Roll
- Futomaki (Thick Roll)
- Dragonfly Roll
- Smoked Salmon Roll
- Tuna Tartare Roll
- Wasabi and Cucumber Roll
- Sweet Potato Tempura Roll
- Tofu and Avocado Roll
- Asparagus and Salmon Roll

- Gyoza Sushi Roll
- Spicy Salmon Roll
- Shrimp and Mango Roll
- Ahi Poke Roll
- Cucumber and Crab Roll
- Blackened Tuna Roll
- Sweet and Sour Shrimp Roll
- Wasabi-Infused Salmon Roll
- Grilled Chicken Teriyaki Roll
- Sushi Burrito
- Crispy Rice Sushi
- Miso-Glazed Salmon Roll
- Salmon and Cream Cheese Roll
- Tuna and Mango Roll
- Prawn and Avocado Nigiri

California Roll
Ingredients:

- 1 cup sushi rice, cooked and seasoned
- 1 sheet nori (seaweed)
- 1/4 cucumber, julienned
- 1/4 avocado, sliced
- 4 oz imitation crab (or real crab meat)
- Soy sauce for dipping

Instructions:

1. Lay the nori on a bamboo sushi mat, shiny side down.
2. Spread a thin layer of rice over the nori, leaving a 1-inch border at the top.
3. Place cucumber, avocado, and crab along the bottom of the rice.
4. Roll the sushi tightly, then slice into pieces.
5. Serve with soy sauce.

Spicy Tuna Roll
Ingredients:

- 1 cup sushi rice, cooked and seasoned
- 1 sheet nori
- 1/2 lb fresh tuna, diced
- 2 tablespoons mayonnaise
- 1 teaspoon sriracha sauce
- 1/4 cucumber, julienned
- Soy sauce for dipping

Instructions:

1. Mix tuna with mayonnaise and sriracha sauce to create a spicy tuna mixture.
2. Lay nori on a sushi mat and spread a thin layer of rice on top.
3. Add cucumber and the spicy tuna mixture.
4. Roll tightly and slice into bite-sized pieces.
5. Serve with soy sauce.

Dragon Roll
Ingredients:

- 1 cup sushi rice, cooked and seasoned
- 1 sheet nori
- 4 oz eel (unagi) or cooked shrimp
- 1/4 avocado, sliced thin
- Cucumber strips
- Eel sauce for drizzling

Instructions:

1. Spread rice on the nori, leaving a small border at the top.
2. Place eel (or shrimp), cucumber, and avocado along the bottom.
3. Roll tightly and slice into pieces.
4. Drizzle with eel sauce and serve.

Rainbow Roll
Ingredients:

- 1 cup sushi rice, cooked and seasoned
- 1 sheet nori
- 1/4 cucumber, julienned
- 1/4 avocado, sliced thin
- Assorted sashimi-grade fish (salmon, tuna, yellowtail, etc.)
- Soy sauce for dipping

Instructions:

1. Lay the nori on the bamboo mat and spread a thin layer of rice.
2. Add cucumber and avocado slices.
3. Top with assorted fish slices to create a "rainbow" effect.
4. Roll tightly, slice, and serve with soy sauce.

Philly Roll
Ingredients:

- 1 cup sushi rice, cooked and seasoned
- 1 sheet nori
- 4 oz smoked salmon
- 1/4 cucumber, julienned
- 1/4 avocado, sliced thin
- Cream cheese (optional)

Instructions:

1. Spread a thin layer of rice on the nori.
2. Place smoked salmon, cucumber, and avocado on top.
3. Add a small dollop of cream cheese if desired.
4. Roll tightly, slice, and serve.

Shrimp Tempura Roll
Ingredients:

- 1 cup sushi rice, cooked and seasoned
- 1 sheet nori
- 2-3 pieces of cooked shrimp tempura
- 1/4 cucumber, julienned
- 1/4 avocado, sliced thin
- Soy sauce for dipping

Instructions:

1. Spread rice evenly on the nori.
2. Place shrimp tempura, cucumber, and avocado in the center.
3. Roll tightly, slice, and serve with soy sauce.

Ebi Nigiri
Ingredients:

- 6 sushi rice balls
- 6 cooked shrimp (ebi), peeled and deveined
- Soy sauce for dipping

Instructions:

1. Shape small rice balls with your hands.
2. Place a piece of cooked shrimp on top of each rice ball.
3. Serve with soy sauce.

Avocado Cucumber Roll

Ingredients:

- 1 cup sushi rice, cooked and seasoned
- 1 sheet nori
- 1/4 cucumber, julienned
- 1/4 avocado, sliced thin
- Soy sauce for dipping

Instructions:

1. Spread rice on the nori, leaving a small border at the top.
2. Add cucumber and avocado slices along the bottom.
3. Roll tightly, slice, and serve with soy sauce.

Spider Roll
Ingredients:

- 1 cup sushi rice, cooked and seasoned
- 1 sheet nori
- Soft-shell crab (fried or cooked)
- 1/4 cucumber, julienned
- 1/4 avocado, sliced thin
- Eel sauce for drizzling

Instructions:

1. Spread rice on the nori.
2. Place the soft-shell crab, cucumber, and avocado on the rice.
3. Roll tightly, slice, and drizzle with eel sauce.

Salmon and Avocado Roll

Ingredients:

- 1 cup sushi rice, cooked and seasoned
- 1 sheet nori
- 4 oz fresh salmon, sliced thin
- 1/4 avocado, sliced thin
- Soy sauce for dipping

Instructions:

1. Spread rice on the nori.
2. Layer with salmon and avocado slices.
3. Roll tightly, slice, and serve with soy sauce.

Veggie Roll
Ingredients:

- 1 cup sushi rice, cooked and seasoned
- 1 sheet nori
- 1/4 cucumber, julienned
- 1/4 avocado, sliced thin
- 1/4 carrot, julienned
- Soy sauce for dipping

Instructions:

1. Spread rice on the nori.
2. Add cucumber, avocado, and carrot along the bottom.
3. Roll tightly, slice, and serve with soy sauce.

Tuna Nigiri
Ingredients:

- 1 cup sushi rice, cooked and seasoned
- 6 slices fresh tuna (sashimi-grade)
- Soy sauce for dipping

Instructions:

1. Shape small rice balls with your hands.
2. Place a slice of fresh tuna on top of each rice ball.
3. Serve with soy sauce for dipping.

Unagi (Grilled Eel) Roll
Ingredients:

- 1 cup sushi rice, cooked and seasoned
- 1 sheet nori
- 4 oz grilled eel (unagi)
- Cucumber, julienned
- Eel sauce for drizzling

Instructions:

1. Spread rice evenly on the nori.
2. Place grilled eel and cucumber in the center.
3. Roll tightly and slice into pieces.
4. Drizzle with eel sauce and serve.

Tempura Shrimp Nigiri
Ingredients:

- 1 cup sushi rice, cooked and seasoned
- 6 pieces of cooked tempura shrimp
- Soy sauce for dipping

Instructions:

1. Shape small rice balls with your hands.
2. Place a piece of tempura shrimp on top of each rice ball.
3. Serve with soy sauce for dipping.

Spider Roll with Soft Shell Crab

Ingredients:

- 1 cup sushi rice, cooked and seasoned
- 1 sheet nori
- 2-3 pieces of soft shell crab (fried)
- Avocado, sliced thin
- Cucumber, julienned
- Eel sauce for drizzling

Instructions:

1. Spread rice on the nori.
2. Place fried soft shell crab, avocado, and cucumber in the center.
3. Roll tightly, slice, and drizzle with eel sauce.

Crispy Shrimp Roll
Ingredients:

- 1 cup sushi rice, cooked and seasoned
- 1 sheet nori
- 4 pieces of crispy shrimp (tempura-style)
- Avocado, sliced thin
- Cucumber, julienned
- Soy sauce for dipping

Instructions:

1. Spread rice on the nori.
2. Place crispy shrimp, avocado, and cucumber on top.
3. Roll tightly, slice, and serve with soy sauce.

Salmon Roe Gunkan Maki

Ingredients:

- 1 cup sushi rice, cooked and seasoned
- 1 sheet nori, cut into strips
- 2 tablespoons salmon roe (ikura)
- Soy sauce for dipping

Instructions:

1. Shape small rice balls with your hands.
2. Wrap a strip of nori around each rice ball, forming a small "boat" shape.
3. Fill the "boat" with salmon roe.
4. Serve with soy sauce for dipping.

Tuna Tataki Roll

Ingredients:

- 1 cup sushi rice, cooked and seasoned
- 1 sheet nori
- 4 oz tuna tataki (seared tuna)
- Avocado, sliced thin
- Soy sauce for dipping

Instructions:

1. Spread rice on the nori.
2. Layer with tuna tataki and avocado slices.
3. Roll tightly, slice, and serve with soy sauce.

Poke Roll

Ingredients:

- 1 cup sushi rice, cooked and seasoned
- 1 sheet nori
- 4 oz poke-grade tuna or salmon, diced
- Cucumber, julienned
- Avocado, sliced thin
- Soy sauce for dipping

Instructions:

1. Spread rice on the nori.
2. Place diced poke-grade fish, cucumber, and avocado on top.
3. Roll tightly, slice, and serve with soy sauce.

Sashimi Salad Roll
Ingredients:

- 1 cup sushi rice, cooked and seasoned
- 1 sheet nori
- Assorted sashimi (tuna, salmon, etc.)
- Mixed salad greens (arugula, spinach, etc.)
- Soy sauce for dipping

Instructions:

1. Spread rice on the nori.
2. Layer with sashimi slices and salad greens.
3. Roll tightly, slice, and serve with soy sauce.

Spicy Crab Roll
Ingredients:

- 1 cup sushi rice, cooked and seasoned
- 1 sheet nori
- 4 oz crab meat (imitation or real)
- 2 tablespoons mayonnaise
- 1 teaspoon sriracha sauce
- Avocado, sliced thin
- Soy sauce for dipping

Instructions:

1. Mix crab meat with mayonnaise and sriracha sauce to create a spicy crab mixture.
2. Spread rice on the nori.
3. Add the spicy crab mixture and avocado slices.
4. Roll tightly, slice, and serve with soy sauce.

Tamago (Japanese Omelette) Nigiri
Ingredients:

- 1 cup sushi rice, cooked and seasoned
- 1 piece of tamago (Japanese sweet omelette), sliced
- Soy sauce for dipping

Instructions:

1. Shape small rice balls with your hands.
2. Place a slice of tamago on top of each rice ball.
3. Serve with soy sauce for dipping.

Yellowtail Roll
Ingredients:

- 1 cup sushi rice, cooked and seasoned
- 1 sheet nori
- 4 oz yellowtail (hamachi), sliced thin
- Avocado, sliced thin
- Soy sauce for dipping

Instructions:

1. Spread rice on the nori.
2. Layer with yellowtail and avocado slices.
3. Roll tightly, slice, and serve with soy sauce.

Maki Roll with Scallops
Ingredients:

- 1 cup sushi rice, cooked and seasoned
- 1 sheet nori
- 4 oz fresh scallops, thinly sliced
- Cucumber, julienned
- Avocado, sliced thin
- Soy sauce for dipping

Instructions:

1. Spread rice evenly over the nori.
2. Place scallops, cucumber, and avocado in the center.
3. Roll tightly, slice, and serve with soy sauce.

Hamachi (Yellowtail) Nigiri

Ingredients:

- 1 cup sushi rice, cooked and seasoned
- 6 slices fresh hamachi (yellowtail), sashimi-grade
- Soy sauce for dipping

Instructions:

1. Shape small rice balls with your hands.
2. Place a slice of yellowtail on top of each rice ball.
3. Serve with soy sauce for dipping.

Salmon Skin Roll

Ingredients:

- 1 cup sushi rice, cooked and seasoned
- 1 sheet nori
- 4 oz grilled salmon skin
- Cucumber, julienned
- Avocado, sliced thin
- Eel sauce for drizzling

Instructions:

1. Spread rice on the nori.
2. Add grilled salmon skin, cucumber, and avocado.
3. Roll tightly, slice, and drizzle with eel sauce.

Crab Stick Roll
Ingredients:

- 1 cup sushi rice, cooked and seasoned
- 1 sheet nori
- 4 oz imitation crab sticks (surimi)
- Cucumber, julienned
- Avocado, sliced thin
- Soy sauce for dipping

Instructions:

1. Spread rice on the nori.
2. Add crab sticks, cucumber, and avocado.
3. Roll tightly, slice, and serve with soy sauce.

Futomaki (Thick Roll)
Ingredients:

- 1 cup sushi rice, cooked and seasoned
- 1 sheet nori
- Assorted fillings: pickled radish, cucumber, avocado, tamago (sweet omelette)
- Soy sauce for dipping

Instructions:

1. Spread rice evenly over the nori.
2. Layer with the assorted fillings.
3. Roll tightly, slice into thick pieces, and serve with soy sauce.

Dragonfly Roll
Ingredients:

- 1 cup sushi rice, cooked and seasoned
- 1 sheet nori
- 4 oz shrimp tempura
- Avocado, sliced thin
- Spicy mayo and eel sauce for drizzling

Instructions:

1. Spread rice on the nori.
2. Add shrimp tempura and avocado.
3. Roll tightly, slice, and drizzle with spicy mayo and eel sauce.

Smoked Salmon Roll
Ingredients:

- 1 cup sushi rice, cooked and seasoned
- 1 sheet nori
- 4 oz smoked salmon, thinly sliced
- Cream cheese, small dollops
- Cucumber, julienned
- Soy sauce for dipping

Instructions:

1. Spread rice evenly over the nori.
2. Layer with smoked salmon, cream cheese, and cucumber.
3. Roll tightly, slice, and serve with soy sauce.

Tuna Tartare Roll
Ingredients:

- 1 cup sushi rice, cooked and seasoned
- 1 sheet nori
- 4 oz fresh tuna, diced
- Avocado, sliced thin
- Soy sauce and sesame oil for seasoning
- Soy sauce for dipping

Instructions:

1. Toss the diced tuna with soy sauce and sesame oil.
2. Spread rice on the nori.
3. Place the tuna tartare and avocado on the rice.
4. Roll tightly, slice, and serve with soy sauce.

Wasabi and Cucumber Roll
Ingredients:

- 1 cup sushi rice, cooked and seasoned
- 1 sheet nori
- 2 teaspoons wasabi paste
- Cucumber, julienned
- Soy sauce for dipping

Instructions:

1. Spread rice evenly over the nori.
2. Spread wasabi paste lightly over the rice.
3. Add cucumber and roll tightly.
4. Slice and serve with soy sauce.

Sweet Potato Tempura Roll
Ingredients:

- 1 cup sushi rice, cooked and seasoned
- 1 sheet nori
- 4 oz sweet potato, thinly sliced and tempura-battered
- Cucumber, julienned
- Avocado, sliced thin
- Soy sauce for dipping

Instructions:

1. Prepare the sweet potato tempura by battering and frying the slices.
2. Spread rice on the nori.
3. Layer with sweet potato tempura, cucumber, and avocado.
4. Roll tightly, slice, and serve with soy sauce.

Tofu and Avocado Roll
Ingredients:

- 1 cup sushi rice, cooked and seasoned
- 1 sheet nori
- 4 oz firm tofu, sliced thin
- 1/2 avocado, sliced
- Soy sauce for dipping

Instructions:

1. Spread rice evenly over the nori.
2. Add thin slices of tofu and avocado in the center.
3. Roll tightly, slice, and serve with soy sauce.

Asparagus and Salmon Roll
Ingredients:

- 1 cup sushi rice, cooked and seasoned
- 1 sheet nori
- 4 oz fresh salmon, sliced
- 2 asparagus spears, blanched
- Soy sauce for dipping

Instructions:

1. Spread rice evenly over the nori.
2. Add a slice of salmon and blanched asparagus in the center.
3. Roll tightly, slice, and serve with soy sauce.

Gyoza Sushi Roll
Ingredients:

- 1 cup sushi rice, cooked and seasoned
- 1 sheet nori
- 4-5 gyoza dumplings (cooked, any filling you prefer)
- Soy sauce for dipping

Instructions:

1. Spread rice evenly over the nori.
2. Place a cooked gyoza in the center.
3. Roll tightly, slice, and serve with soy sauce.

Spicy Salmon Roll
Ingredients:

- 1 cup sushi rice, cooked and seasoned
- 1 sheet nori
- 4 oz fresh salmon, diced
- 1 teaspoon sriracha sauce
- 1/2 teaspoon mayo
- Soy sauce for dipping

Instructions:

1. Mix diced salmon with sriracha and mayo for the spicy filling.
2. Spread rice evenly over the nori.
3. Add the spicy salmon mixture in the center.
4. Roll tightly, slice, and serve with soy sauce.

Shrimp and Mango Roll
Ingredients:

- 1 cup sushi rice, cooked and seasoned
- 1 sheet nori
- 4 cooked shrimp, peeled and deveined
- 1/4 mango, thinly sliced
- Soy sauce for dipping

Instructions:

1. Spread rice evenly over the nori.
2. Add shrimp and mango slices in the center.
3. Roll tightly, slice, and serve with soy sauce.

Ahi Poke Roll
Ingredients:

- 1 cup sushi rice, cooked and seasoned
- 1 sheet nori
- 4 oz ahi tuna, diced
- 1 teaspoon soy sauce
- 1 teaspoon sesame oil
- 1/2 teaspoon green onions, sliced
- Soy sauce for dipping

Instructions:

1. Toss the diced ahi tuna with soy sauce, sesame oil, and green onions.
2. Spread rice evenly over the nori.
3. Add the ahi poke mixture in the center.
4. Roll tightly, slice, and serve with soy sauce.

Cucumber and Crab Roll
Ingredients:

- 1 cup sushi rice, cooked and seasoned
- 1 sheet nori
- 4 oz imitation crab sticks (surimi)
- 1/2 cucumber, julienned
- Soy sauce for dipping

Instructions:

1. Spread rice evenly over the nori.
2. Add crab sticks and cucumber in the center.
3. Roll tightly, slice, and serve with soy sauce.

Blackened Tuna Roll
Ingredients:

- 1 cup sushi rice, cooked and seasoned
- 1 sheet nori
- 4 oz tuna, blackened with seasoning
- Avocado, sliced thin
- Soy sauce for dipping

Instructions:

1. Spread rice evenly over the nori.
2. Add slices of blackened tuna and avocado in the center.
3. Roll tightly, slice, and serve with soy sauce.

Sweet and Sour Shrimp Roll
Ingredients:

- 1 cup sushi rice, cooked and seasoned
- 1 sheet nori
- 4 cooked shrimp, peeled and deveined
- 1 tablespoon sweet and sour sauce
- Cucumber, julienned
- Soy sauce for dipping

Instructions:

1. Toss the shrimp in sweet and sour sauce.
2. Spread rice evenly over the nori.
3. Add shrimp and cucumber in the center.
4. Roll tightly, slice, and serve with soy sauce.

Wasabi-Infused Salmon Roll
Ingredients:

- 1 cup sushi rice, cooked and seasoned
- 1 sheet nori
- 4 oz fresh salmon, sliced
- 1/2 teaspoon wasabi paste
- Soy sauce for dipping

Instructions:

1. Spread rice evenly over the nori.
2. Thinly spread wasabi paste on the salmon slices.
3. Place the salmon in the center of the nori.
4. Roll tightly, slice, and serve with soy sauce.

Grilled Chicken Teriyaki Roll
Ingredients:

- 1 cup sushi rice, cooked and seasoned
- 1 sheet nori
- 4 oz grilled chicken breast, thinly sliced
- 1 tablespoon teriyaki sauce
- Soy sauce for dipping

Instructions:

1. Drizzle teriyaki sauce over the grilled chicken slices.
2. Spread rice evenly over the nori.
3. Place the chicken in the center.
4. Roll tightly, slice, and serve with soy sauce.

Sushi Burrito
Ingredients:

- 1 cup sushi rice, cooked and seasoned
- 1 large sheet nori
- 4 oz cooked shrimp or fish of your choice
- 1/4 avocado, sliced
- 1/2 cucumber, julienned
- Soy sauce for dipping

Instructions:

1. Spread rice evenly over the entire sheet of nori.
2. Layer shrimp or fish, avocado, and cucumber in the center.
3. Roll tightly into a burrito shape, slice, and serve with soy sauce.

Crispy Rice Sushi
Ingredients:

- 1 cup sushi rice, cooked and seasoned
- 1/2 cup rice flour
- Vegetable oil for frying
- 4 oz sushi-grade tuna, thinly sliced
- Soy sauce for dipping

Instructions:

1. Form sushi rice into small rectangular cakes.
2. Dust rice cakes lightly with rice flour.
3. Fry them in hot oil until golden and crispy.
4. Top each rice cake with a slice of tuna.
5. Serve with soy sauce.

Miso-Glazed Salmon Roll
Ingredients:

- 1 cup sushi rice, cooked and seasoned
- 1 sheet nori
- 4 oz fresh salmon, grilled and miso-glazed
- 1/2 cucumber, julienned
- Soy sauce for dipping

Instructions:

1. Spread rice evenly over the nori.
2. Add the grilled, miso-glazed salmon in the center.
3. Place cucumber slices beside the salmon.
4. Roll tightly, slice, and serve with soy sauce.

Salmon and Cream Cheese Roll
Ingredients:

- 1 cup sushi rice, cooked and seasoned
- 1 sheet nori
- 4 oz smoked salmon
- 2 tablespoons cream cheese
- Fresh dill for garnish
- Soy sauce for dipping

Instructions:

1. Spread rice evenly over the nori.
2. Add smoked salmon and a dollop of cream cheese in the center.
3. Garnish with fresh dill.
4. Roll tightly, slice, and serve with soy sauce.

Tuna and Mango Roll
Ingredients:

- 1 cup sushi rice, cooked and seasoned
- 1 sheet nori
- 4 oz fresh tuna, sliced
- 1/4 mango, julienned
- Soy sauce for dipping

Instructions:

1. Spread rice evenly over the nori.
2. Layer fresh tuna and mango in the center.
3. Roll tightly, slice, and serve with soy sauce.

Prawn and Avocado Nigiri
Ingredients:

- 1 cup sushi rice, cooked and seasoned
- 4 cooked prawns
- 1/2 avocado, sliced
- Soy sauce for dipping

Instructions:

1. Shape the sushi rice into small, oval-shaped portions.
2. Place a slice of avocado and a prawn on top of each rice portion.
3. Serve with soy sauce.

www.ingramcontent.com/pod-product-compliance
Lightning Source LLC
LaVergne TN
LVHW081503060526
838201LV00056BA/2910